creative crafts from
cardboard
boxes

By Nikki Connor

Illustrated by
Sarah-Jane
Neaves

Copper Beech Books
Brookfield, Connecticut

© Aladdin Books Ltd 1996
Designed and produced by
Aladdin Books Ltd
28 Percy Street
London W1P 0LD

First published in the United States
in 1996 by
Copper Beech Books,
an imprint of
The Millbrook Press
2 Old New Milford Road
Brookfield, Connecticut 06804

Design David West Children's Book
Design
Illustrator Sarah-Jane Neaves
Photographer Roger Vlitos

Printed in Belgium

Library of Congress Cataloging-in-
Publication Data.

Connor, Nikki Cardboard Boxes / by Nikki
Connor : illustrated by Sarah-Jane Neaves.
    p. cm. -- (Creative crafts from)
    Summary: Provides
instructions for a variety of craft projects
for young children using cardboard boxes.
    ISBN 0-7613-0538-6 (lib. bdg.). --
    ISBN 0-7613-0513-0 (pbk.) 1. Box craft--
Juvenile literature. 2. Paperback--Juvenile
literature. [1. Box craft. 2. Handicraft.]
I. Neaves, Sarah-Jane, ill. II. Title. III. Series.
TT870.5.C66   1996   96-12639
745.54--dc20   CIP AC

Contents

Before you start

A "what you need" ingredients panel appears with the photograph of each project. Decide which project you are going to make and collect everything you need.

 The red, yellow, and blue paint cups mean that you need poster paints. All colors (except white) can be made by mixing together a combination of these three. See the color chart at the back of this book to find out how. You may choose instead to use ready mixed colors if you have them.

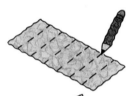  Use a pencil point to punch holes in paper or thin cardboard. For holes in thicker cardboard and in plastic, use scissors - <u>adult help is needed for this.</u>

A dotted line in the instructions means you are to fold, not cut. A solid line shows where to cut.

Only use scissors that are especially designed for children's crafts. They usually have rounded ends. Always have an adult with you when you use them.

Where a project needs colored paper remember you may use any color you choose. If you have none, use white paper and paint it!

If you follow the step-by-step instructions carefully you will be sure to finish up with a successful model - but if you prefer to use these designs just as ideas to get you started, then that's fine too!

Have fun.

train

adhesive tape

scissors

paintbrush

cardboard boxes

poster paints

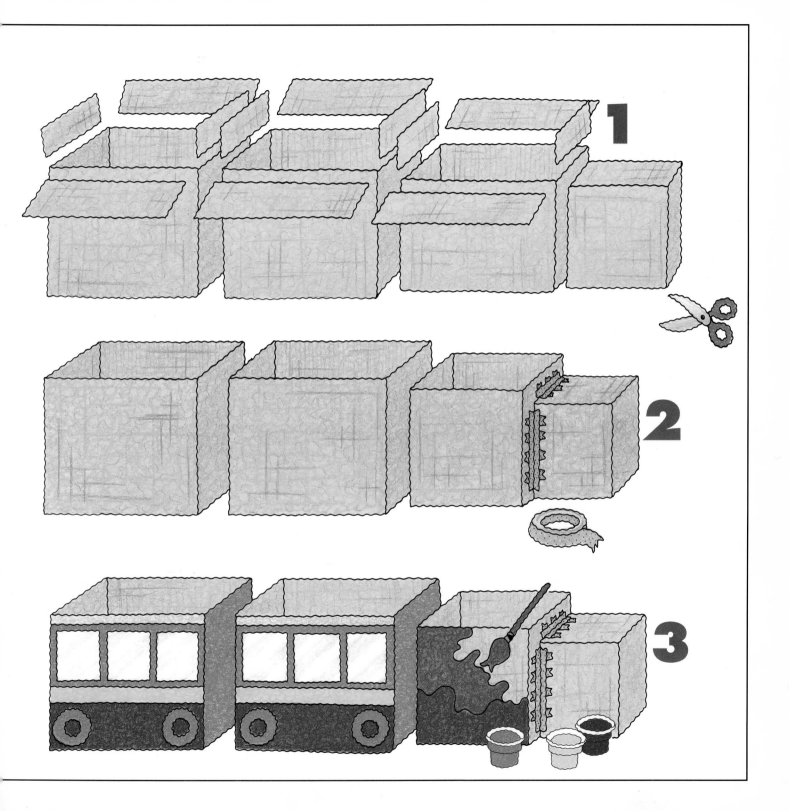

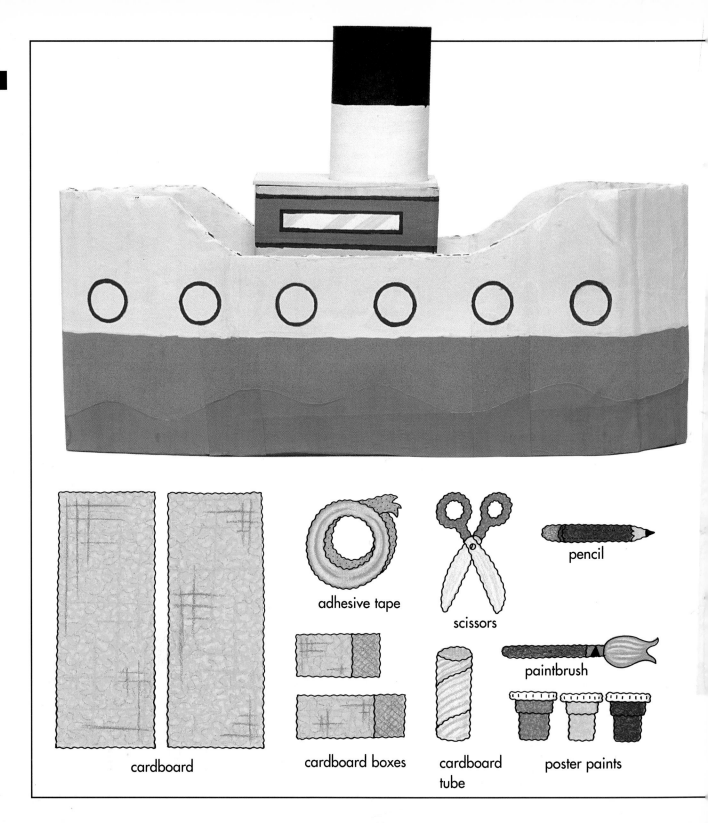

ship

cardboard

adhesive tape

scissors

pencil

cardboard boxes

cardboard tube

paintbrush

poster paints

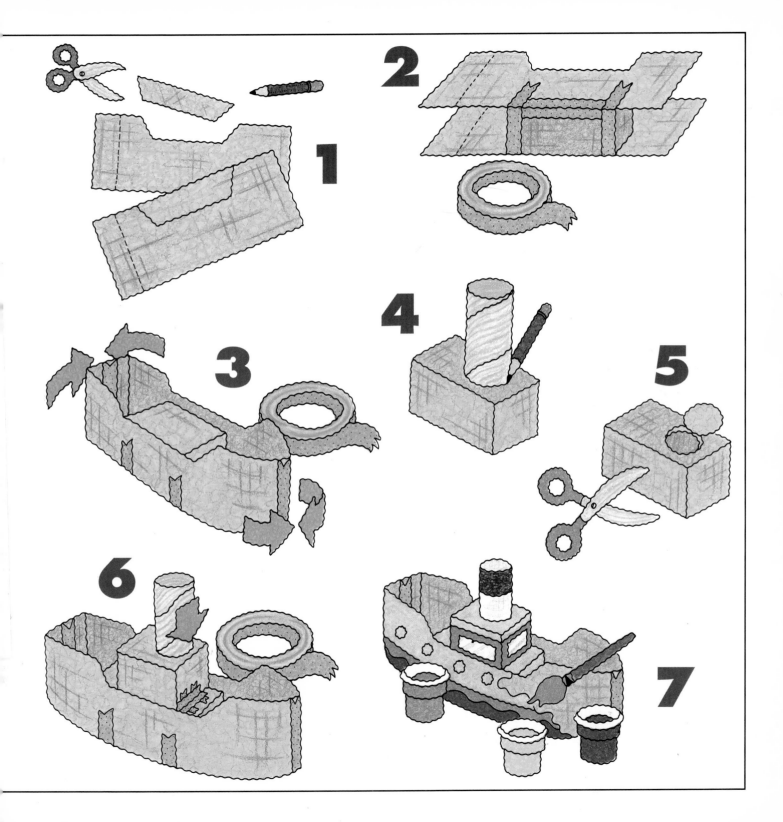

car

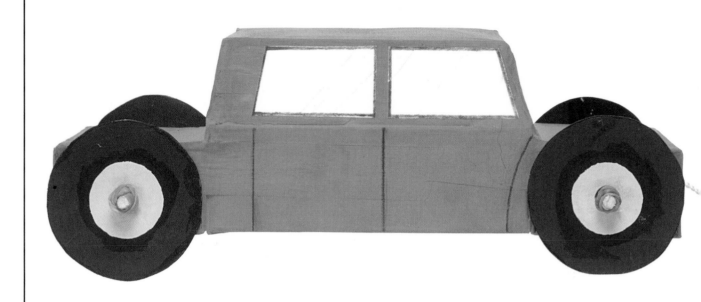

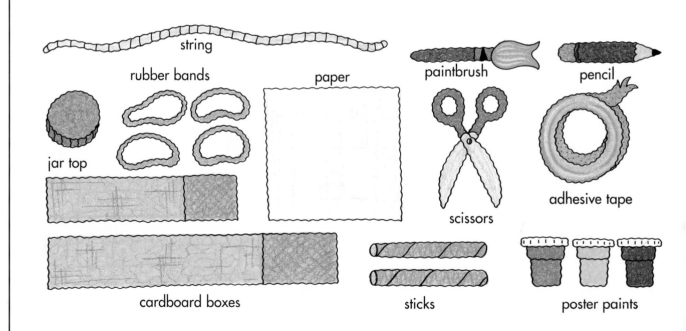

string

rubber bands

paper

paintbrush

pencil

jar top

scissors

adhesive tape

cardboard boxes

sticks

poster paints

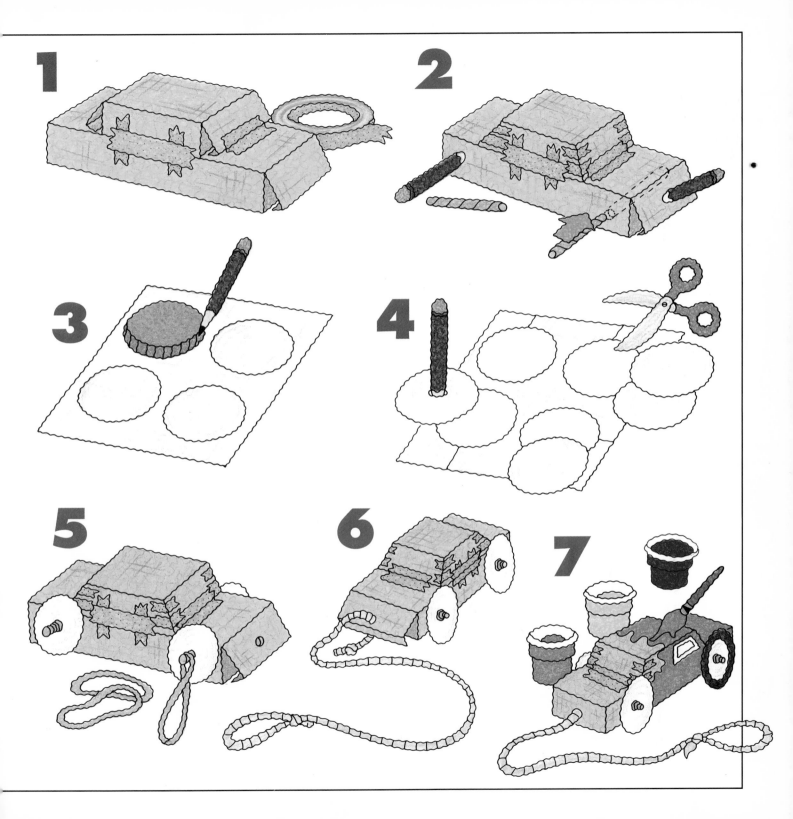

1

2

3

4

5

6

7

clock

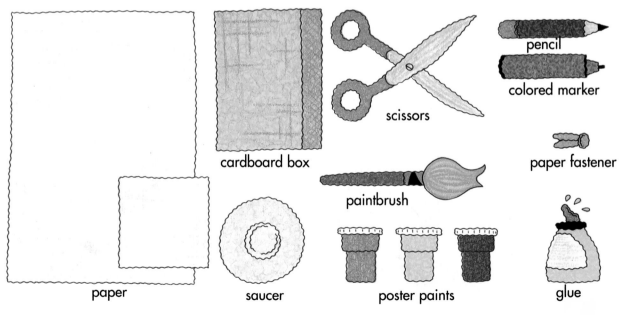

paper

cardboard box

scissors

pencil

colored marker

paper fastener

saucer

paintbrush

poster paints

glue

shoes

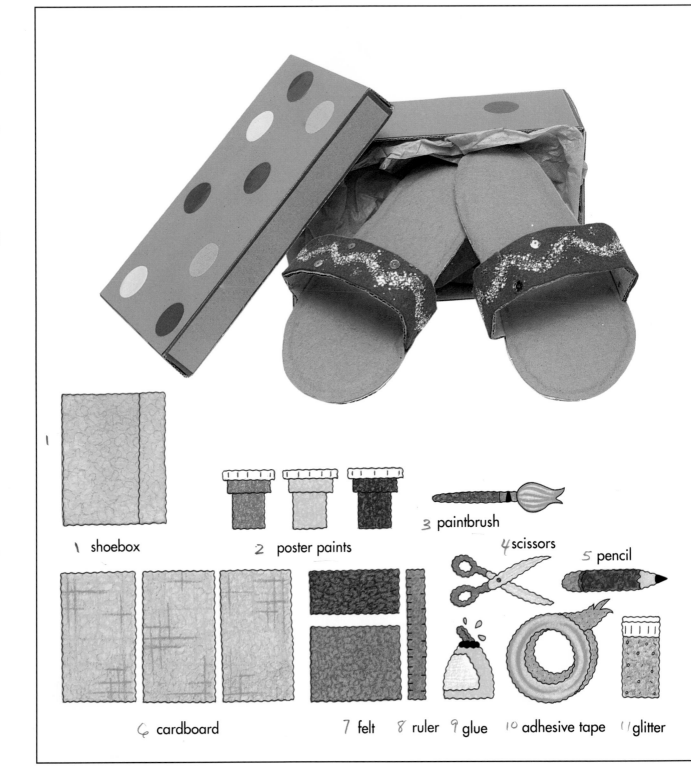

1 shoebox

2 poster paints

3 paintbrush

4 scissors

5 pencil

6 cardboard

7 felt   8 ruler   9 glue   10 adhesive tape   11 glitter

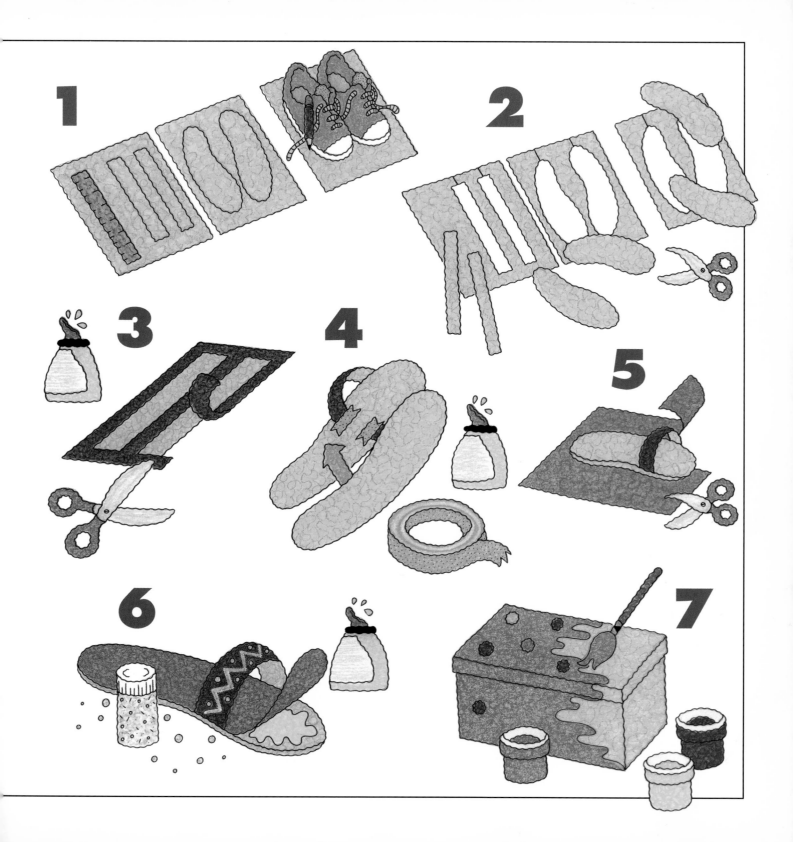

puppet theater

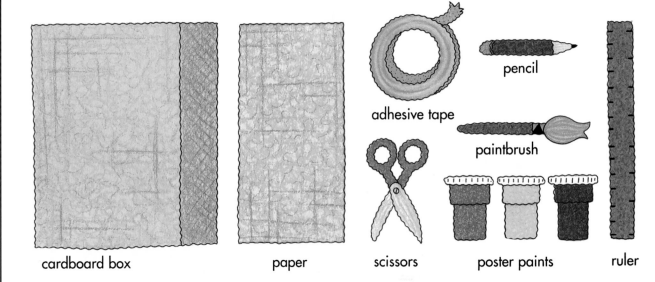

cardboard box   paper   scissors   poster paints   ruler

adhesive tape   pencil

paintbrush

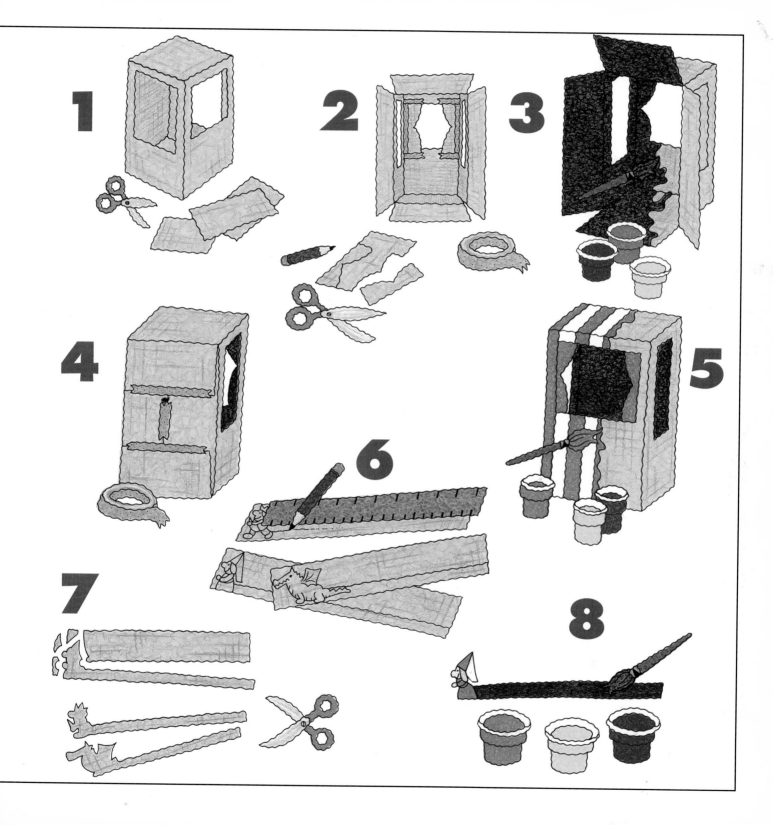

cardboard box

pencil

scissors

paper

glue

sticks

adhesive tape

paintbrush

poster paints

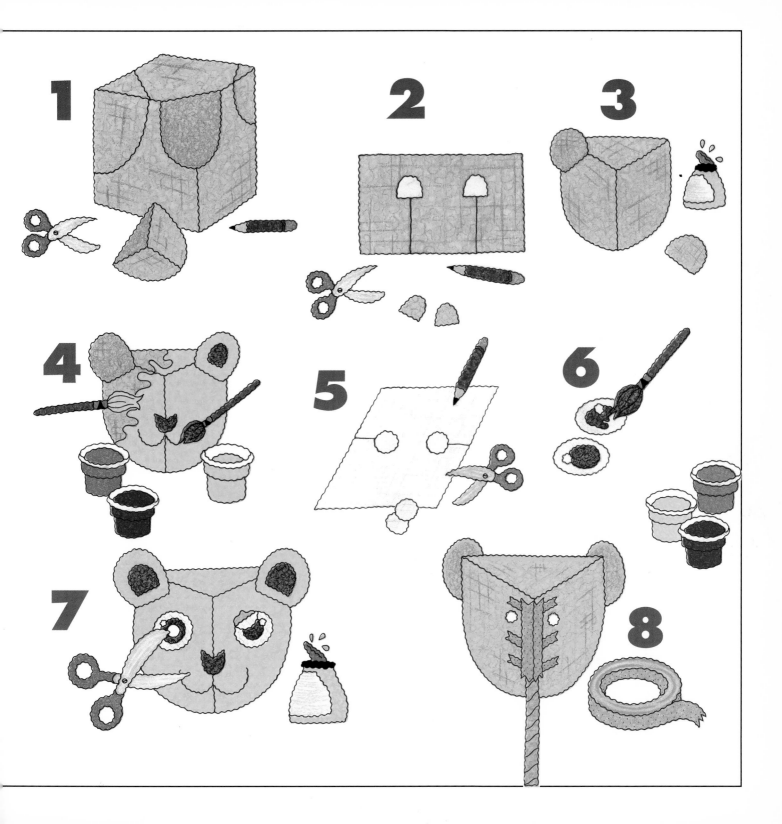

castle

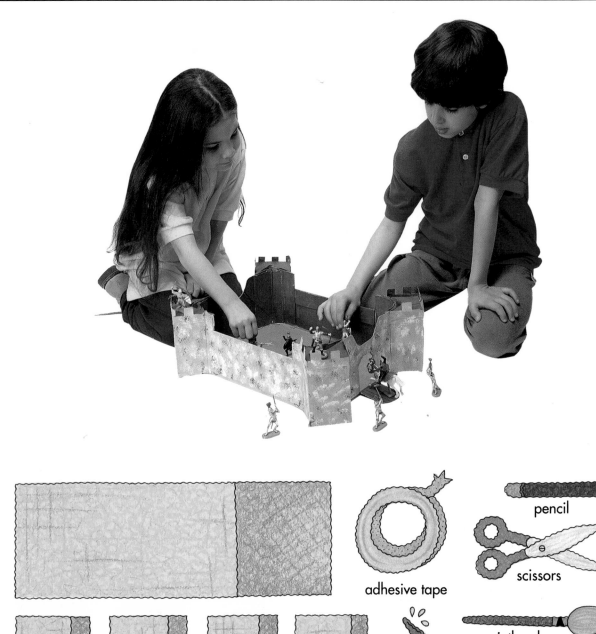

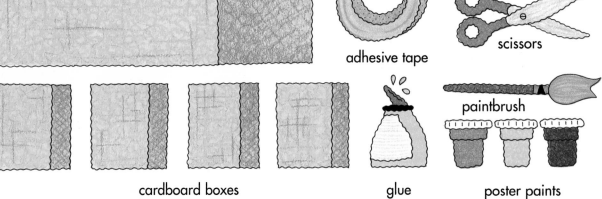

cardboard boxes

adhesive tape

pencil

scissors

paintbrush

glue

poster paints

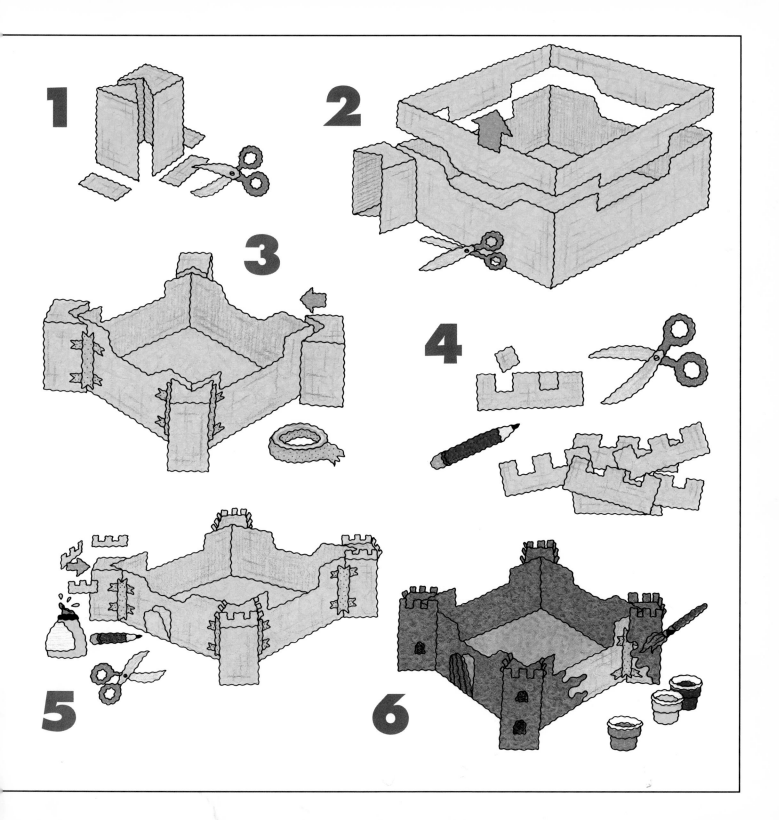

rainforest

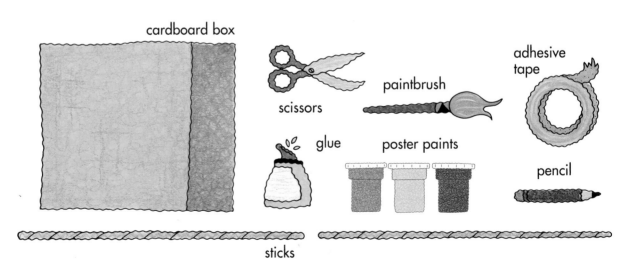

cardboard box

scissors

paintbrush

adhesive tape

glue

poster paints

pencil

sticks

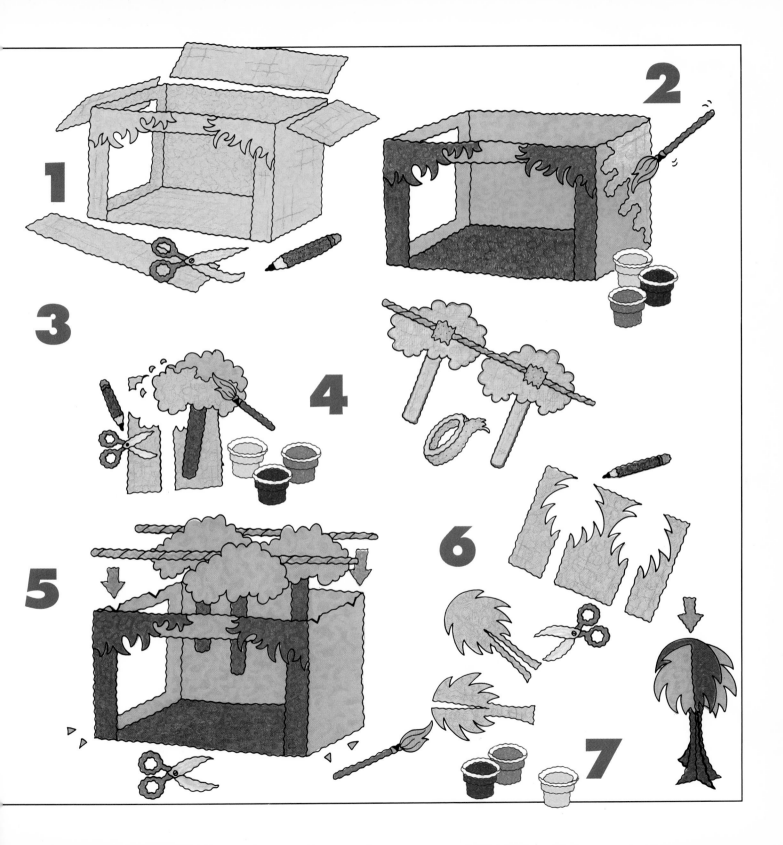

doll's house

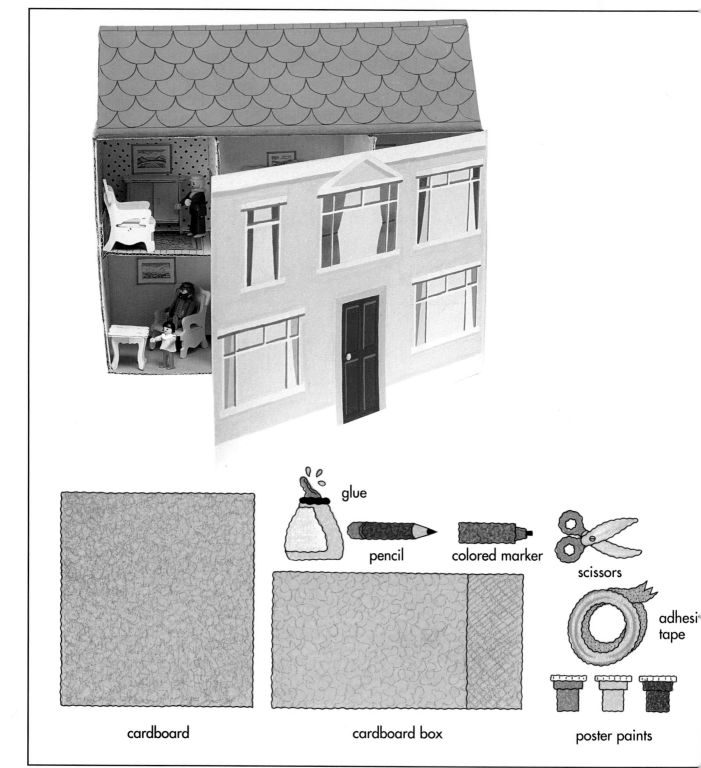

cardboard

glue

pencil

colored marker

scissors

adhesive tape

cardboard box

poster paints

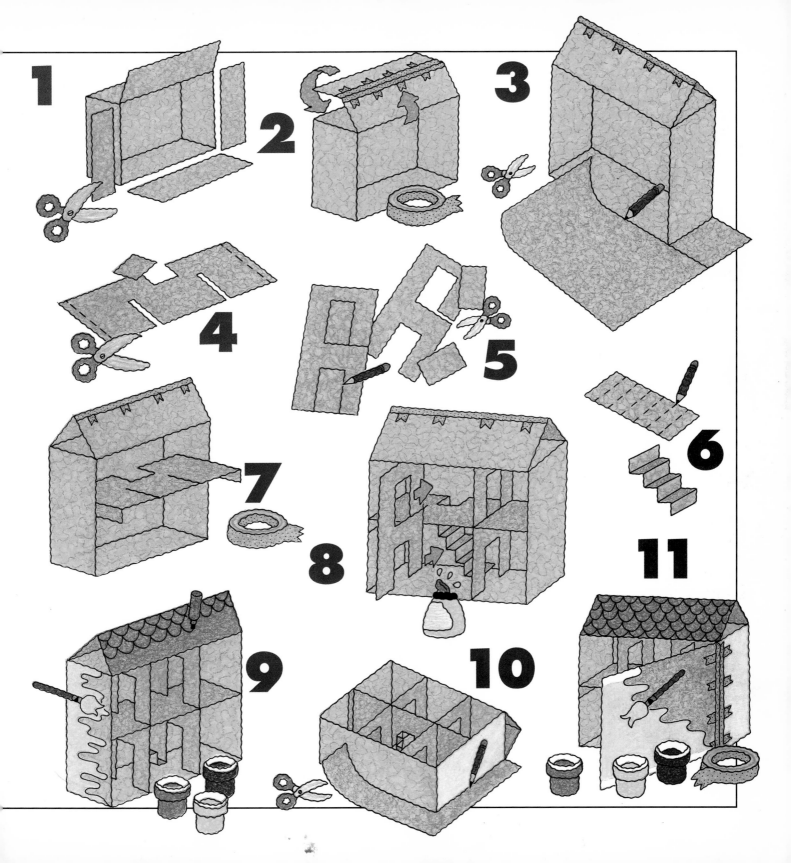

color chart

You can mix the three primary colors to make all the colors of the rainbow. Follow the chart below to mix the colors you want. The numbers on the cups show the proportions of each color you need to make the new color.

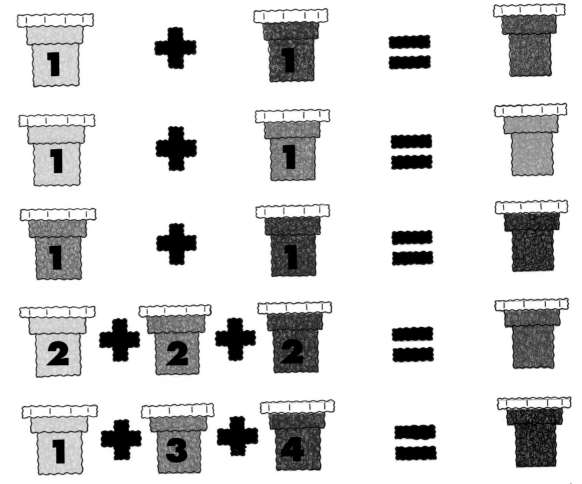

Different types of paint will give different results. Experiment by mixing different proportions of colors. Make sure you wash the brush before dipping it into each paint cup.